Cheerleading

by Jill Sherman

BLASTOFF! READERS
2

BELLWETHER MEDIA · MINNEAPOLIS, MN

Note to Librarians, Teachers, and Parents:

Blastoff! Readers are carefully developed by literacy experts and combine standards-based content with developmentally appropriate text.

Level 1 provides the most support through repetition of high-frequency words, light text, predictable sentence patterns, and strong visual support.

Level 2 offers early readers a bit more challenge through varied simple sentences, increased text load, and less repetition of high-frequency words.

Level 3 advances early-fluent readers toward fluency through increased text and concept load, less reliance on visuals, longer sentences, and more literary language.

Level 4 builds reading stamina by providing more text per page, increased use of punctuation, greater variation in sentence patterns, and increasingly challenging vocabulary.

Level 5 encourages children to move from "learning to read" to "reading to learn" by providing even more text, varied writing styles, and less familiar topics.

Whichever book is right for your reader, Blastoff! Readers are the perfect books to build confidence and encourage a love of reading that will last a lifetime!

This edition first published in 2020 by Bellwether Media, Inc.

No part of this publication may be reproduced in whole or in part without written permission of the publisher. For information regarding permission, write to Bellwether Media, Inc., Attention: Permissions Department, 6012 Blue Circle Drive, Minnetonka, MN 55343.

Library of Congress Cataloging-in-Publication Data

Names: Sherman, Jill, author.
Title: Cheerleading / by Jill Sherman.
Description: Minneapolis, MN : Bellwether Media, Inc., 2020. | Series: Blastoff! Readers : Let's Play Sports! | Audience: Ages 5-8. | Audience: Grades K-3. | Includes bibliographical references and index.
Identifiers: LCCN 2018058733 (print) | LCCN 2019002696 (ebook) | ISBN 9781618915399 (ebook) | ISBN 9781600149993 (hardcover : alk. paper)
Subjects: LCSH: Cheerleading–Juvenile literature. | Cheers–Juvenile literature.
Classification: LCC LB3635 (ebook) | LCC LB3635 .S54 2019 (print) | DDC 791.6/4–dc23
LC record available at https://lccn.loc.gov/2018058733

Text copyright © 2020 by Bellwether Media, Inc. BLASTOFF! READERS and associated logos are trademarks and/or registered trademarks of Bellwether Media, Inc. SCHOLASTIC, CHILDREN'S PRESS, and associated logos are trademarks and/or registered trademarks of Scholastic Inc., 557 Broadway, New York, NY 10012.

Editor: Rebecca Sabelko   De

Printed in the United States of A

Table of Contents

What Is Cheerleading?	4
What Are the Rules for Cheerleading?	10
Cheerleading Gear	18
Glossary	22
To Learn More	23
Index	24

Cheerleading is a sport that includes cheering, dancing, **stunts**, and much more!

Cheerleaders work together as a team. Teams are also called squads.

stunt

4

cheerleading competition

Some cheer squads are **competitive**. They do their **routines** for judges.

They earn points for **difficulty**, skill, and new ideas.

Other cheer squads use their skills to cheer on other sports teams.

Kentucky Wildcats

Champion Spotlight
University of Kentucky Wildcats Cheerleading

- Division 1A college cheerleading
- Accomplishments:
  - Won Universal Cheerleaders Association's (UCA) College Cheerleading National Championship 24 times
  - Only team to have won 8 years in a row between 1995 and 2002

They often cheer for football and basketball teams from the sidelines. They get the fans excited!

What Are the Rules for Cheerleading?

Cheerleading squads do routines with many stunts and dances.

They jump and kick.
They move into **formations**.

Formations have three
positions. Bases lift and
toss the flyer into the air.

flyer

spotter

bases

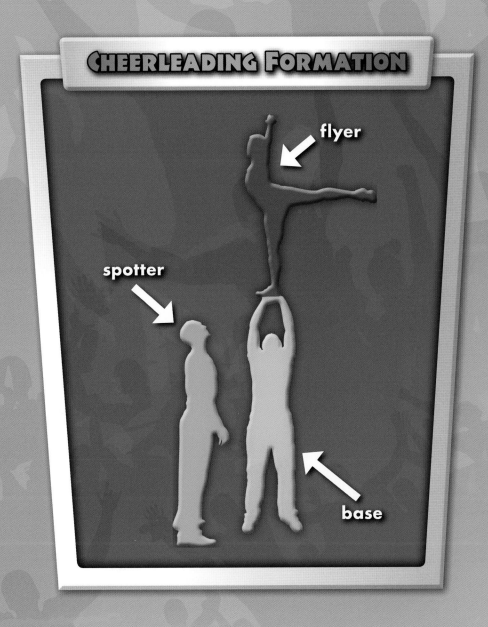

Cheerleading Formation

flyer

spotter

base

Flyers do tricks. Spotters
make sure everyone is safe.

Difficult stunts and jumps earn points for competitive teams.

Cheerleaders complete many stunts. They do flips and **cartwheels**. They try to do each move perfectly!

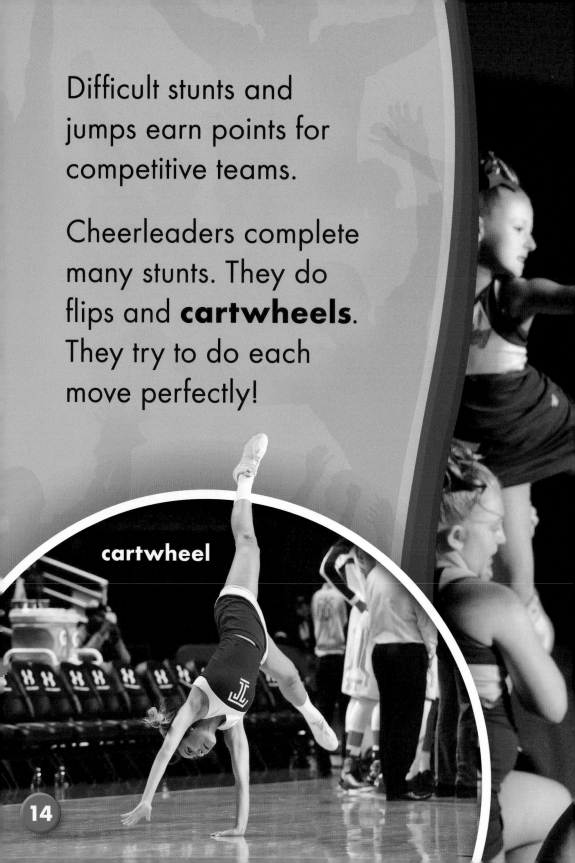

cartwheel

Judges score the routines.
They give points for
different moves.

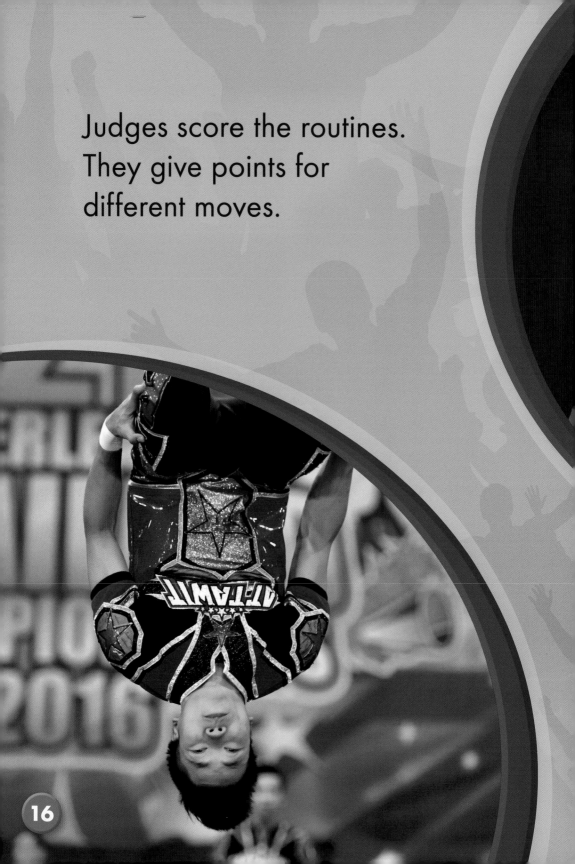

They **deduct** points for falls.
The team with the most
points wins!

Cheerleading Gear

Cheerleaders dress for success.
They wear uniforms in their
school or squad colors.

Cheerleaders wear **athletic** shoes to help with jumping and tumbling.

CHEERLEADING GEAR

athletic shoes   megaphones

pom-poms   uniforms

Cheerleaders wave bright **pom-poms** in the air. They shout into **megaphones**.

Cheer squads get the crowd roaring!

megaphones

pom-pom

Glossary

athletic—related to sports

cartwheels—sideways movements done by placing one hand and then the other on the ground, before lifting the feet into the air and landing on one foot before the other

competitive—a cheerleading squad who tries to win against another squad

deduct—to take away from something

difficulty—how hard it is to do something

formations—groups of cheerleaders who create specific shapes

megaphones—large cones used to make voices louder

pom-poms—round balls of colored streamers

routines—actions that a group follows for a performance

stunts—types of cheerleading movements that take skill

To Learn More

Duling, Kaitlyn. *Cheerleading*. Minneapolis, Minn.: Bullfrog Books, 2018.

Gassman, Julie. *Cheerleading Really Is a Sport*. Mankato, Minn.: Stone Arch Books, 2011.

Yomtov, Nel. *Being Your Best at Cheerleading*. New York, N.Y.: Children's Press, 2017.

ON THE WEB

FACTSURFER

Factsurfer.com gives you a safe, fun way to find more information.

1. Go to www.factsurfer.com.

2. Enter "cheerleading" into the search box and click 🔍.

3. Select your book cover to see a list of related web sites.

Index

bases, 12
cartwheels, 14
cheering, 4, 8, 9
colors, 18
dancing, 4, 10
deduct, 17
falls, 17
fans, 9
flips, 14
flyer, 12, 13
formations, 11, 12, 13
gear, 19
judges, 6, 16
jump, 11, 14, 19
Kentucky Wildcats, 8, 9
kick, 11
megaphones, 20
points, 7, 14, 16, 17

pom-poms, 20, 21
routines, 6, 10, 16
shoes, 19
sidelines, 9
spotters, 12, 13
squads, 4, 6, 8, 10, 18, 20
stunts, 4, 10, 14
team, 4, 8, 9, 14, 17
tumbling, 19
uniforms, 18

The images in this book are reproduced through the courtesy of: DaydreamsGirl, front cover (cheerleader); Think A, front cover (background field); Aspen Photo, pp. 4 (inset), 14 (inset); Imageplotter News and Sports/ Alamy, pp. 4-5; Chatchai Somwat/ Alamy, pp. 6-7 (top), 16 (bottom); Aija Lehtonen, p. 7 (bottom); Icon Sportswire/ Getty, pp. 8-9; David Banks/ Getty, pp. 10-11 (top); Krabikus, p. 12, 19 (athletic shoes); Xinhua/ Alamy, pp. 14-15; dov makabaw sundry/ Alamy, pp. 16-17 (top); By View Apart, pp. 18-19 (top); Kristen Prahl, pp. 19 (megaphone), 20 (inset); Richard Paul Kane, p. 19 (pom-poms); Portland Press Herald/ Getty, p. 19 (uniforms); The Washington Post/ Getty, pp. 20-21.